THE AMISH COUNTRY

GALLERY BOOKS
An Imprint of W. H. Smith Publishers Inc.
112 Madison Avenue
New York City 10016

This edition first published in U.S.
in 1991 by Gallery Books,
an imprint of W.H. Smith Publishers, Inc.
112 Madison Avenue, New York, New York 10016

ISBN 0-8317-0259-1

Printed and bound in Spain

For rights information about the photographs in
this book please contact:

The Image Bank
111 Fifth Avenue, New York, NY 10003

Producer: Solomon M. Skolnick
Writer: Bob Brooke
Design Concept: Lesley Ehlers
Designer: Ann-Louise Lipman
Editor: Sara Colacurto
Production: Valerie Zars
Photo Researcher: Edward Douglas
Assistant Photo Researcher: Robert V. Hale
Editorial Assistant: Carol Raguso

Title page: A statue of a stoic Amish farmer stands outside Zinn's Diner near Reading, Pennsylvania. The statue is a landmark in this part of Amish country. *Opposite:* The average Amish farm is 55 acres, a size that allows farmers to till the fields by hand.

Neatly painted homesteads dot the countryside. Most possess a windmill, its spinning wheel a contrast to the angular fields of corn and alfalfa. The barns, tobacco sheds, and houses stand crisp in the morning light, free of electric wires. White wooden fences outline pastures, and the land looks like a giant quilt of neat rectangles rich in earthen tones. A gray-covered buggy, pulled by a horse clip-clopping against the road, breaks the morning stillness. Although it is the twentieth century, time seems to have stood still in the eighteenth century here, for this is Amish country.

Just like the purple martins that fill the multi-roomed bird-houses in their front yards, the Amish are a communal group, plain and simple. Both share a common need to live near their own. But the Amish are not the only "plain folk" that live in Amish country.

About 16,000 Old Order people live in the area around Lancaster, Pennsylvania. They migrated to the United States from Germany and Switzerland in the 1720's and represent the oldest Amish settlements in 20 U.S. states and one Canadian province. In all, there are over 47,000 Amish, with the largest group living in Holmes and Wayne counties in Ohio, the destination of a second migration from Europe in the nineteenth century. With an average of seven new settlements founded each year, the Amish population nearly doubles every 20 years.

Old Order Amish use horse-drawn buggies for transportation. *Overleaf:* Amish carriages travel past neatly painted Amish farmsteads outside Lancaster, Pennsylvania.

In Amish country there are strong sentiments attached to the use of land and animals, time and energy, because the Amish believe these are gifts from God. *Below:* The Amish pull together to help each other in the greater community, as in this barn-raising for a neighbor in Lancaster County. *Opposite:* To the Amish, buggies are not old-fashioned; they are simply the only mode of transportation Old Order beliefs permit them to own.

In Apple Creek, Ohio, an Old Order Amish farmer plows his fields behind a team of four steady horses, as his ancestors have done for hundreds of years. *Below:* Though their beliefs do not permit them to use tractors, many Amish farmers do use modern farm equipment – pulled by animals. *Opposite:* A reliable cash crop for the Amish is that of tobacco, fields of which are planted and harvested by hand by members of the family regardless of age, as seen on this Richland, Pennsylvania, farm.

The first Amish arrived in Lancaster County from Europe in the early 1700's to escape religious persecution and to take part in William Penn's "Holy Experiment" of religious freedom. In Europe, they were originally part of a larger group, the Anabaptists, who believed in adulthood baptism and congregated under the leadership of Dutch Catholic priest Menno Simons. Simons' Anabaptist followers were more specifically known as Mennonites. It was not until 1697, a century-and-a-half after the establishment of the Mennonites' permanent doctrine, that Jacob Amman, also a Dutch Mennonite, founded his own group, which would adhere more to the founding beliefs and practices of the Old Order.

One of these practices, still in use today, was the social avoidance of anyone expelled from the church. Such shunning, known as *meidung*, means not traveling, doing business, or eating with a former church member. Amman's followers of this strict practice, as well as other Old Order practices, became known as the Amish.

Today, the Anabaptists make up three groups—the Amish, Mennonites, and Brethren. The differences among the seven Amish, 21 Mennonite, and nine Brethren groups lie in their interpretation of the Bible, their use of modern technology (or lack thereof), the value they place on education, their use of English, and their degrees of interaction with outsiders. Brethren and Mennonite groups make use of modern conveniences more than Old Order Mennonites and Amish sects, particularly the Old Order Amish, who shun modern technology completely.

A typical Amish farm has at least six horses and mules to pull the field implements used for cultivation.

The Amish can be recognized by their clothing. It is said that they wear their religion, unlike the Catholics and Protestants. The clothing they wear today is similar to that worn by their ancestors during the seventeenth and eighteenth centuries.

The manner in which the Amish dress and groom themselves symbolizes their role in Amish society. Men wear several different styles of hats that represent different ages, status in the community, and the group of Amish to which they belong. They must begin to grow a beard when they are married, a custom that was once practiced upon baptism. They wear black hats in the winter and straw ones in the summer.

Amish women wear full-length dresses, capes, and aprons. Those that have been baptized wear white organdy caps and do not cut their hair. In the winter the women wear black bonnets for warmth.

Buttons are used to fasten men's pants and shirts, but coats and vests are closed with hooks and eyes, since buttons on these outer garments might be considered decoration, a forbidden feature for Amish clothing. They are, however, seen on sweaters and work coats.

These standards of dress, as well as those of home decorating, transportation, and farm practice, are all included in the *Ordnung*, the unwritten rules of each church district. Borderline matters are often discussed at a semiannual meeting of ministers and bishops. It is important that agreement and peace abide in the community before the members have communion once each spring and fall. At these Sunday services, those who have been baptized and are in

Preceding page: Corn is a low-energy, high-yield crop for the Amish farmer and serves as fodder for his livestock. Tobacco, on the other hand, is a crop so labor-intensive that a family with even as many as six to eight children seldom plants more than five acres. *This page:* A tobacco barn stands next to a field of corn in Lancaster County. The hinged panels on the barn's sides are set open to provide proper ventilation for the drying crop. *Right:* An Amish farmer will chop a third of his corn acreage into silage and let the rest dry for shell and ear corn. *Overleaf:* Corncribs, ventilated structures used for storing ears of corn, stand out in the crisp light of late winter on an Amish farm.

"good standing" take a bit of bread broken from a slice cut from a homemade loaf and a swallow of wine. Afterwards, members wash each other's feet, an act which symbolizes loving service towards one another.

Regular church services are held every other Sunday in one of the 20 to 35 households that geographically make up the church district. All of the households are close enough that members can travel easily for worship. Amish families spend alternate Sundays resting or visiting, doing only essential work, such as milking the cows.

There are many preparations for a family hosting the church or "preaching" service, as the Amish call their biweekly worship. An Amish house is designed with folding or sliding doors separating the rooms on the first floor. These must be opened and the whole floor cleaned. During the week before the service, an enclosed horse-drawn cart delivers backless benches that are set up in rows for the service.

Church is a full-day event, beginning with the singing of at least two songs before one of the ministers gives the *Anfang,* or short sermon. He speaks in Pennsylvania Dutch but quotes scripture in High German. This is followed by silent prayer and comments, and a chapter of the Bible is read by the deacon. The main sermon is an hour of biblical interpretation by a minister. The same minister then reads a prayer from *Christenpflicht,* which means "Christian's duty."

Top to bottom: The incidence of highway accidents involving buggies is on the rise as urbanization creeps into once rural Amish country. A gathering of buggies in Shipshewana, Indiana, could just as easily be in Pennsylvania or Ohio, two other U.S. states with large Amish populations. Reflective triangles on the backs of buggies warn motorists to keep their distance and be patient, so as not to scare the horses.

In Lancaster County, the most often used color for Amish buggies is gray. Across the United States, however, buggies in black, white, and yellow are often seen. *Overleaf:* Amish farmsteads are meticulously maintained, from the neatly painted buildings, to the carefully planted rows of crops, to the beautifully manicured flower gardens.

Preceding page: A group of horse and buggies parked outside an Amish home in Shipshewana indicates that a worship service is being held there. *This page:* Buggies of relatives and friends gather at an Amish cemetery in St. Jacobs, Ontario, Canada. *Below:* A brief service is held at the cemetery after the home funeral, as the relatives and friends of the deceased gather at the graveside. *Overleaf:* Gray buggies line the lawn of an Amish farmhouse in Lancaster County on Sunday morning; the Amish take turns hosting worship services, which take place every other week.

On church day, the host family serves the same menu as that of the other host families, so there is no competition. The meal consists of at least 30 *snitz* pies, each filled with dried apples, made from scratch the day before. Other foods, usually cold, are bologna, pickled red beets, and homemade cup cheese, all served with coffee. Several families usually bring homemade bread to be spread with a mixture of molasses and peanut butter.

The men sit at one table and the women at another. The older folks eat first, and then the tables are filled and refilled with other guests until everyone has been served.

Being together is a top priority for the Amish, since they cannot communicate by phone. Invitations for any event are delivered in person whenever possible. Each person tends to socialize within his or her peer group, in which news from other Amish settlements is shared.

Farming is primarily how the Amish make their living. Farm tasks demand full-time input from the whole family. While caring for crops and animals, parents are able to show their children how to live and make a living without exposure to influences that would confuse or contradict their beliefs.

Top to bottom: An Amish farmwife uses utensils handed down from her mother, or reproductions of older ones; the only decorative items are those which are also useful. Although this is a model country store, actual ones still serve Amish communities around Lancaster. The Amish are known for their fine wood craftsmanship, and farmers make items during the idle days of winter to sell to tourists and non-Amish neighbors. *Opposite:* The Heritage Center Museum in Lancaster (top) displays decorative arts of the Amish, such as quilts and furniture of the late eighteenth and nineteenth century. The Southern Market (bottom) was once a farmers market, but now it's used as the head-quarters for the Lancaster County Chamber of Commerce.

Preceding page: Mill Bridge Village in Lancaster County offers a glimpse of Amish life with buggy rides, quilt shops, and local foods. *This page:* The farmhouse of the Landis Valley Museum in Lancaster County is just part of the largest museum of Pennsylvania German rural life in the United States. *Below:* Mill Bridge Village features a charming colonial mill village with an operating mill, dating from 1728, and working craftsmen.

In this way, the farm becomes a setting for religious nurture as well as an enterprise that provides for the basic needs of the family members.

The Amish believe that land, time, and energy are gifts of God. They view land as a source of nourishment for people and take great care of it to maximize its productivity. Time—especially daylight time—offers an important opportunity to care for the family and the land. An Amish farmer depends on the sun more than any other energy source.

The average Amish farm is only 55 acres, much smaller than most tractor-operated farms in the United States but often just as productive. Through crop rotation, stripping, and the use of hybrid seed, the Amish have learned to produce as much on 50 acres as was once produced on 100. The Amish farmer has become a master of timing, meeting the needs of each crop and keeping his horses and equipment effectively maintained.

The farm implements of the Old Order Amish are mended antiques or copies of pre-World War II models. Keeping them functioning requires careful maintenance. However, the Amish believe that running a self-sufficient farm by family cooperation and without government aid is the way to build integrity.

One of the most conspicuous crops grown by the Amish is tobacco. When the leaves are mature in September, whole families take to the fields to cut stalks with shears and spear them onto 48-inch lathes, which are then hung on a specially built wagon frame. Lifting a full lathe weighing at least 25 pounds is known as "heavy work." On each farm, tobacco leaves can be seen hanging in rows from floor to ceiling in the tobacco shed.

A former harness-racing horse briskly pulls a buggy through the Amish countryside.

Evening darkness is a time for slowing down and gathering the family together under a propane gas lamp before retiring early. In many families, the school-age children are roused between four and five o'clock in the morning to help with the milking of the cows before breakfast and classes. In the heat and warmth of the night-time kitchen, family members grant each other privacy within their togetherness. They sew, read, or write letters with no other illumination save the hissing lamp that draws them inside an enclosing brightness.

The Amish home is a place of silence—for being and for thinking —filled with varied scents. Inside, the aroma of drying tobacco wafts in from an open shed, mingling with the pungent aroma of grapes cooking for jelly. The clock on the kitchen shelf chimes, the only interruption in an otherwise still room. The windows sparkle and are covered by simple green shades, the only window dressing allowed. The wooden floors, shined from constant cleaning, are covered with handmade Amish rag carpets.

An Amish home uses limited fossil energy. The kitchen lacks electric-powered appliances (and electrical outlets), and the stove and refrigerator are converted to run on bottled gas. Floors are swept and washed rather than vacuumed.

A lot of living goes on in an Amish farmhouse. Up to four generations may be born on the same property. Most farmhouses have an addition, called a *grosdaddihaus*, meaning "grandfather's house," built for use by the parents when their children marry.

Amish boys play on the porch of a one-room schoolhouse, where they are taught reading, writing, arithmetic, geography, history, and music.

Amish schools have only eight grades. The school day begins with the singing of hymns, Bible readings, and the Lord's prayer.

Wearing Amish clothing just like their parents', two Amish youngsters play on a trampoline in front of their home. *Below:* Amish children, who usually have to tend to schoolwork and chores, enjoy washing the family buggy on Saturday.

The Amish live in large, though simple, farmhouses without electricity that often have an addition for the grandparents; all have lush gardens that bloom throughout the summer. *Below:* A high population-growth rate and the soaring price of land have forced the Amish to establish cottage industries on their farms; this one sells handmade quilts to visitors. *Opposite:* Young girls learn the skills of homemaking, like baking bread, at an early age so they can help their mothers with the chores.

An Amish family's canning cellar holds a winter's supply of preserved fruits and vegetables. *Left:* An immaculate wood-burning stove is the centerpiece of an Amish kitchen and the pride of an Amish farmwife. *Opposite:* An Amish farmer readies a game of chess to pass the long winter evenings.

Births usually occur in the house, where an Amish family welcomes the newborn with warmth but little fanfare. There are no ceremonies to mark the occasion—no baby showers, no religious dedications. When the baby is about to be born, the husband leaves his farmwork to contact the midwife or doctor and direct the household. The grandmother, or *grosmommy*, comes to take care of the newborn and the other children.

The Amish view children as a gift from the Lord and their young are carefully nurtured throughout their early years. From infancy, children go wherever the family goes, wear Amish clothes, and learn to speak the Pennsylvania German dialect. Such boundaries form a strong Amish identity.

Preschoolers learn early to show respect for authority and to take on family responsibility. Grownups expect a child to obey and include the young ones in family activities, meals, and group work such as pea-shelling; a five-year-old child may be expected to take a container down the road to a neighbor either by foot or by wagon. Skill in handling a team of horses develops over the years, but youngsters often practice by pretending to hitch up their playmates.

Top to bottom: A bright, handmade quilt adorns a farmhouse bed; the residents' Sunday clothes hang on hooks on the wall. An Amish bedroom is simple and unadorned; here, black mourning clothes, which must be worn for up to a year, are laid out for the funeral of a relative. The clothing the Amish wear today, in varying shades of blue, lavender, red, and sometimes pale green, is similar to that worn by their ancestors during the seventeenth and eighteenth centuries. *Opposite:* There are several different styles of hats distinguishing different ages, status in the community, and the group of Amish the wearer belongs to. Black hats are worn in the winter and straw ones in the summer.

Growing up Amish is very important to being truly Amish. Offspring follow the ways of their parents in the generational cycle; they call this keeping the faith. The patterns of life and the work habits that support these people are ingrained in each child. When a child questions actions by "English" people, or those of the larger society, a parent will often say, "This is *unserer weg* (our way)." Amish children gain a sense of belonging from working hard. They feel needed, and as a result the family develops a strong bond.

Education is very important in the Amish community. The bell that the teacher rings signaling the beginning of each school day is probably the same one that was heard by several generations. In the one-room Amish schools there is also a sense of continuity.

When the bell rings, the children quickly hang up their jackets on hooks in the anteroom and all the "scholars" (as the Amish call their students), from first to eighth grade, scramble into wooden school desks. The room has only the barest necessities: a woodstove, with a teakettle to heat water for washing hands in a basin before lunch; a peg for each drinking cup; and rods above the stove with clothespins attached to dry gloves in winter. Arriving at 8:30 A.M., pupils will stay here until the end of the school day at 3:30 P.M.

Most teachers in Amish schools are the product of the Amish school system. Children attend school only through the eighth grade, and girls who show teaching ability are tapped for work as teachers later on. Their skills come mostly from intuition and experience.

For Amish children, telling time, doing practical math problems, and writing legibly are the most important results of an education, for these are the skills they will most depend on later in life. Since the Amish do not use

telephones, they must communicate by writing letters, which are delivered by friends or by mail.

Sixteen is a landmark age for Amish children. Amish youth begin "running around" at that age, which means joining a group or "supper gang." This group of 150 to 200 older teens meets on Sundays to play games and sing. Driving his own horse and buggy, a boy may take his sister as far as 20 miles—a two-and-one-half-hour ride—to the home where a family has invited the gang for afternoon volleyball or softball. Only the boys play, while the girls chatter and admire from the sidelines and then serve a treat of perhaps lemonade and pretzels.

Amish society derives strength from age-group associations. All the girls who turn 16 in one year become a "buddy bunch." These girls often become close friends, eventually attending each others' weddings.

Dating is allowed at age 16, but many Amish youth spend two or more years socializing with the "gang" before a boy singles out a specific girl. After the Sunday-night singings, a boy might drive a special girl home; eventually he will spend other Sunday evenings visiting at her home. Curfews are not an issue when dating. It is not unusual for a young man to return from a visit near dawn.

Preceding pages: Amish clothing hung out to dry on wash day reveals that the clothing of both adults and children is identical. *Opposite:* Amish children are allowed to play in the park just as other kids do. *Below:* When a young man is about 16 years old, he is given an open buggy, which he may use for courting.

The Amish have a strong sense of community with strong bonds between families. The young are taught to respect their elders. *Opposite:* An Amish family visits the local grocery store in a small town outside Lancaster to buy food. *Overleaf:* Amish girls who turn age 16 in the same year form a "buddy bunch," becoming close friends and eventually attending each others' weddings.

In the Amish community, the teenage years are a time for tasting the world. Some young men secretly buy cars or try drinking, but usually they do it as an act. A girl may exercise her adolescent independence by making her bedroom fancy with candles, artificial flowers, and dishes.

Weddings are undoubtedly the highlight of the Amish social scene. After fall communion at church, a young couple's wedding date is announced or "published" during Sunday-morning preaching.

November is the wedding month among the Amish. Traditionally held on Tuesdays or Thursdays, weddings are sometimes attended by as many as 400 guests. Women arrive several days early to help prepare the prescribed food: whole roasted chickens, mounds of flavorful stuffing, mashed potatoes with gravy, cole slaw, bread with butter and jam, and celery cooked in a delicate sweet-sour sauce. It is a sure sign that a wedding is approaching when extra celery is planted in the garden of a family with a marriageable daughter. Dessert features apple pie with whipped cream, a berry sauce, cookies, cream-filled doughnuts, canned peaches, and coffee.

The wedding ceremony lasts three hours and begins with an hour of singing by those assembled. Afterwards, the bride and groom and their attendants come from upstairs to hear two sermons and exchange their vows.

Friday is usually market day for the Amish, however, men often attend livestock and equipment sales held on Mondays. *Below:* Amish farmers partake of some roast pig at a local market. *Opposite:* House and farm sales are well attended by the Amish, who buy old tools and such to use on their farms.

Newly married Amish couples have no honeymoon. Instead, they spend several weeks visiting relatives before settling down in their own homes. With most life events happening at home, the Amish family is the core of the community's strength. The extended family rallies to help when an accident or handicap hinders others in the district. Church members always depend on each other before they turn to non-Amish institutions.

A high population-growth rate and the soaring price of land around them have forced the Amish to look for income alternatives to farming. Many have taken to opening small cottage industries and make carriages, clocks, batteries, silos, cabinets, quilts, and toys. Their construction expertise is now often sought for fine home building.

To the Amish, beauty is its own ornament. A good example of this is the quilt. A quilt begins as a way for frugal Amish housewives to use leftover scraps of cloth and ends as an expression of happiness and a work of art.

Quilting was not always an Amish tradition. It was adopted from their "English" neighbors in the nineteenth century, and ever since Amish women have pieced together their patchwork designs on treadle sewing machines. Early on, girls learn to cut out bars, squares, triangles, and such from cardboard patterns. Certain patterns are standard, but each maker varies the colors and the border to make her own unique quilt. Years ago, the Amish used only the colors they wore — magenta, purple, lavender, forest green, and robin-egg blue — but today, they use almost any color.

Bright orange pumpkins decorate the exterior of this country store in Intercourse, Pennsylvania.

The Amish accept death as a part of life. The community absorbs the departure of a loved one as quietly as it does the birth of a child. Funerals are also prescribed and have not changed in decades. Just about everything is done by family and friends, which keeps the cost down.

Funerals are held at the home of the deceased, and at least 300 people attend. A simple six-sided coffin is used, and the first floor of the house is opened up to accept guests. As with other Amish events, the menu is standard: sliced cold beef with hot gravy and mashed potatoes, cheese cut in squares, bread with molasses-and-peanut-butter spread, and finally home-canned fruit.

Amish society emphasizes informal learning-through-doing; a life of "goodness," rather than a life of intellect; wisdom, rather than technical knowledge; community welfare, rather than competition; and separation, rather than integration with contemporary world society. On the whole, these qualities have not been altered through the centuries. But as a people, the Amish, like other cultures, do change. Although their ways more often withstand the persecution that threatens their "separateness," they are flexible on matters that do not tamper with family solidarity and their integrity. They are a proud people and have chosen to face the future rather than shrink from it.

Top to bottom: The Old Country Store on Main Street in Intercourse is laden with articles from more than 450 local craftspersons, including these colorful quilts and stuffed toys. Quilting and doll-making are an assumed tradition for an Amish girl; these examples are displayed for sale in Bird-in-Hand, Pennsylvania. Many Amish farms earn extra money by producing decorative drafts to sell to visitors, such as these hand-painted milk cans. *Opposite:* Traditional Amish quilts are geometric in design; this *Disselfink* bird design is an adaptation of the original.

Preceding page: Ever since the Amish adopted quilting from their "English" neighbors in the nineteenth century, they have pieced their patchwork designs together on treadle sewing machines; these women are holding up a quilt at an auction in Millersberg, Ohio. *This page:* Before a quilt can be sewn together, cardboard patterns must be cut out of material scraps in the shapes of bars, squares, diamonds, rectangles, triangles, and petals.

The *Double Wedding Ring* pattern is unusual among Amish quilt patterns, since most Amish quilts are of designs based on rectilinear forms.

Certain quilt patterns have become standard, such as this *World Without End* pattern.

Quilting stitches often follow the route of the *piecework*, the templates of cardboard or plastic used to mark the pattern in the open areas; in this quilt of *Touching Stars*, the stitches are repeated in the same pattern as the patches.

This *Bars* pattern is one of the most basic and popular for use on Amish bedcovers; this one has the wide border and subtle colors found in most Amish designs.

The artistic quality of a quilt is determined by the colors, how the corners of the piecework meet, and whether the quilting is even. *Opposite:* Baptized Amish women wear white organdy caps and do not cut their hair; in winter they wear black bonnets for warmth.

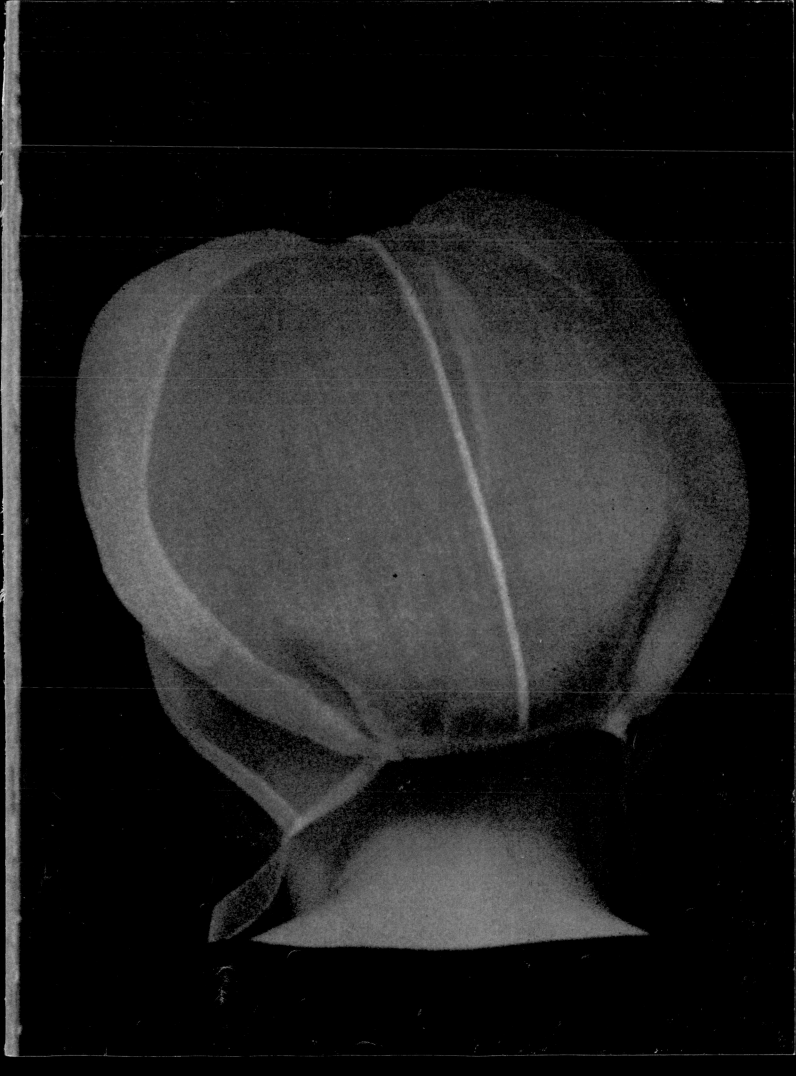

Index of Photography

TIB indicates The Image Bank